Tertullian
De Spectaculis

Tertullian
De Spectaculis

Tertullian
De Spectaculis

© Lighthouse Publishing 2018

All rights reserved. Without limiting the rights under copyright reserved above, no part of this publication may be reproduced, stored in a retrieval system, or transmitted, in any form or by any means (electronic, mechanical, photocopying, recording or otherwise), without the prior written permission of the copyright owner of this book.

Published by
Lighthouse Christian Publishing
SAN 257-4330
5531 Dufferin Drive
Savage, Minnesota, 55378
United States of America

www.lighthousechristianpublishing.com

Tertullian

Introductory Note.

[a.d. 145–220.] When our Lord repulsed the woman of Canaan (Matt. xv. 22) with apparent harshness, he applied to her people the epithet *dogs*, with which the children of Israel had thought it piety to reproach them. When He accepted her faith and caused it to be recorded for our learning, He did something more: He reversed the curse of the Canaanite and showed that the Church was designed "for all people;" Catholic alike for all time and for all sorts and conditions of men.

Thus the North-African Church was loved before it was born: the Good Shepherd was gently leading those "that were with young." Here was the charter of those Christians to be a Church, who then were Canaanites in the land of their father Ham. It is remarkable indeed that among these pilgrims and strangers to the West the first elements of Latin Christianity come into view. Even at the close of the Second Century the Church in Rome is an inconsiderable, though prominent, member of the great confederation of Christian Churches which has its chief seats in Alexandria and Antioch, and of which the entire Literature is Greek. It is an African presbyter who takes from Latin Christendom the reproach of theological and literary barrenness and begins the great work in which, upon his foundations, Cyprian and Augustine built up, with incomparable genius, that Carthaginian School of Christian thought by which Latin Theology was dominated for centuries. It is important to note (1.) that providentially not one of these illustrious doctors died in Communion with the Roman See, pure though it was and venerable at that time; and (2.) that to the works of Augustine the Reformation in Germany and Continental Europe was largely due; while (3.) the *specialties* of the Anglican Reformation were, in like proportion, due to the writings of Tertullian and Cyprian. The hinges of great and controlling destinies for Western Europe and our own America are to be found in the period we are now approaching.

The merest school-boy knows much of the history of Carthage, and how the North Africans became Roman citizens. How they became Christians is not so clear. A melancholy destiny has enveloped Carthage from the outset, and its glory and greatness as a Christian See were transient indeed. It blazed out all at once in Tertullian, after about a century of missionary labours had been exerted upon its creation: and having given a Minucius Felix, an Arnobius and a Lactantius to adorn the earliest period of Western Ecclesiastical learning, in addition to its nobler luminaries, it rapidly declined. At the beginning of the Third Century, at a council presided over by Agrippinus, Bishop of Carthage, there were present not less than seventy bishops of the Province. A period of cruel persecutions followed, and the African Church received a baptism of blood.

Tertullian was born a heathen, and seems to have been educated at Rome, where he probably practiced as a jurisconsult. We may, perhaps, adopt most of the ideas of Allix, as conjecturally probable, and assign his birth to a.d. 145. He became a Christian about 185, and a presbyter about 190. The period of his strict orthodoxy very nearly expires with the century. He lived to an extreme old age, and some suppose even till a.d. 240. More probably we must adopt the date preferred by recent writers, a.d. 220.

It seems to be the fashion to treat of Tertullian as a Montanist, and only incidentally to celebrate his services to the Catholic Orthodoxy of Western Christendom. Were I his biographer I should reverse this course, as a mere act of justice, to say nothing of gratitude to a man of splendid intellect, to whom the filial spirit of Cyprian accorded the loving tribute of a disciple, and whose genius stamped itself upon the very words of Latin theology, and prepared the language for the labors of a Jerome. In creating the Vulgate, and so lifting the Western Churches into a position of intellectual equality with the East, the latter as well as St. Augustine himself were debtors to Tertullian in a degree not to be estimated by any other than the Providential Mind that inspired his brilliant career as a Christian.

In speaking of Tatian I laid the base for what I wished to say of Tertullian. Let God only be their judge; let us gratefully recognize the debt we owe to them. Let us read them, as we read the works of King Solomon. We must, indeed, approve of the discipline of the Primitive Age, which allowed of no compromises. The Church was struggling for existence, and could not permit any man to become her master. The more brilliant the intellect, the more dangerous to the poor Church were its perversions of her Testimony. Before the heathen tribunals, and in the market-places, it would not answer to let Christianity appear double tongued. The orthodoxy of the Church, not less than her children, was undergoing an ordeal of fire. It seems a miracle that her Testimony preserved its unity, and that heresy was branded as such by the instinct of the Faithful. Poor Tertullian was cut off by his own act. The weeping Church might bewail him as David mourned for Absalom, but like David, she could not give the Ark of God into other hands than those of the loyal and the true. I have set the writings of Tertullian in a natural and logical order, so as to aid the student, and to relieve him from the distractions of such an arrangement as one finds in Oehler's edition. Valuable as it is, the practical use of it is irritating and confusing. The reader of that edition may turn to the slightly differing schemes of Neander and Kaye, for a theoretical order of the works; but here he will find a classification which will aid his inquiries. He will find, first, those works which connect with the Apologists of the former volumes of this series: which illustrate the Church's position toward the outside world, the Jews as well as the Gentiles. Next come those works which contend with internal differences and heresies. And then, those which reflect the morals and manners of Christians. These are classed with some reference to their degrees of freedom from the Montanistic taint, and are followed, last of all, by the few tracts which belong to the melancholy period of his lapse, and are directed against the Church's orthodoxy.

Let it be borne in mind, that if this sad close of Tertullian's career cannot be extenuated, the later history of Latin Christianity forbids us to condemn him, in the tones which proceeded from the Virgin Church with authority, and which the law of her testimony and the instinct of self-preservation forced her to utter. Let us reflect that St. Bernard and after him the Schoolmen, whom we so deservedly honor, separated themselves far more absolutely than ever Tertullian did from the orthodoxy of Primitive Christendom. The schism which withdrew the West from Communion with the original seats of Christendom, and from Nicene Catholicity, was formidable beyond all expression, in comparison with Tertullian's entanglements with a delusion which the See of Rome itself had momentarily patronized. Since the Council of Trent, not a theologian of the Latins has been free from organic heresies, compared with which the fanaticism of our author was a trifling aberration. Since the late Council of the Vatican, essential Montanism has become organized in the Latin Churches: for what are the new revelations and oracles of the pontiff but the *deliria* of another claimant to the voice and inspiration of the Paraclete? Poor Tertullian! The sad influences of his decline and folly have been fatally felt in all the subsequent history of the West, but, surely subscribers to the Modern Creed of the Vatican have reason to "speak gently of *their father's* fall." To Döllinger, with the "Old Catholic" remnant only, is left the right to name the Montanists heretics, or to upbraid Tertullian as a lapser from Catholicity.

From Dr. Holmes, I append the following Introductory Notice:

(I.) Quintus Septimius Florens Tertullianus, as our author is called in the mss. of his works, is thus noticed by Jerome in his *Catalogus Scriptorum Ecclesiasticorum:* "Tertullian, a presbyter, the first Latin writer after Victor and Apollonius, was a native of the province of Africa and city of Carthage, the son of a proconsular centurion: he was a man of a sharp and vehement temper, flourished under Severus and Antoninus Caracalla, and wrote numerous works, which (as they are generally known) I think it unnecessary to particularize. I saw at Concordia, in Italy, an old man named Paulus. He said that when young he had met at Rome with an aged amanuensis of the blessed Cyprian, who told him that Cyprian never passed a day without reading some portion of Tertullian's works, and used frequently to say, *Give me my master*, meaning Tertullian. After remaining a presbyter of the church until he had attained the middle age of life, Tertullian was, by the envy and contumelious treatment of the Roman clergy, driven to embrace the opinions of Montanus, which he has mentioned in several of his works under the title of the New Prophecy....He is reported to have lived to a very advanced age, and to have composed many other works which are not extant." We add Bishop Kaye's notes on this extract, in an abridged shape: "The correctness of some parts of this account has been questioned. Doubts have been entertained whether Tertullian was a presbyter, although these have solely arisen from Roman Catholic objections to a married priesthood; for it is certain that he was married, there being among his works two treatises addressed to his wife....Another question has been raised respecting the place where Tertullian officiated as a presbyter—whether at Carthage or at Rome. That he at one time resided at Carthage may be inferred from Jerome's statement, and is rendered certain by several passages of his own writings. Allix supposes that the notion of his having been a presbyter of the Roman Church owed its rise to what Jerome said of the envy and abuse of the Roman clergy impelling him to espouse the party of Montanus. Optatus, and the author of the work *de Hæresibus*, which Sirmond edited under the title of Prædestinatus, expressly call him a Carthaginian presbyter. Semler, however, in a dissertation inserted in his edition of Tertullian's works, contends that he was a presbyter of the Roman Church. Eusebius tells us that he was accurately acquainted with the Roman laws, and on other accounts a distinguished person at Rome. Tertullian displays, moreover, a knowledge of the proceedings of the Roman Church with respect to Marcion and Valentinus, who were once members of it, which could scarcely have been obtained by one who had not himself been numbered amongst its presbyters Semler admits that, after Tertullian seceded from the church, he left and returned to Carthage. Jerome does not inform us whether Tertullian was born of Christian parents, or was converted to Christianity. There are passages in his writings which seem to imply that he had been a Gentile; yet he may perhaps mean to describe, not his own condition, but that of Gentiles in general, before their conversion. Allix and the majority of commentators understand them literally, as well as some other passages in which he speaks of his own infirmities and sinfulness. His writings show that he flourished at the period specified by Jerome—that is, during the reigns of Severus and Antoninus Caracalla, or between the years a.d. 193 and 216; but they supply no precise information respecting the date of his birth, or any of the principal occurrences of his life. Allix places his birth about 145 or 150; his conversion to Christianity about a.d. 185; his marriage about 186; his admission to the priesthood about 192; his adoption of the opinions of Montanus about 199; and his death about a.d. 220.

But these dates, it must be understood, rest entirely on conjecture."

(II.) Tertullian's work against Marcion, as it happens, is, *as to its date*, the best authenticated—perhaps the only well authenticated—particular connected with the author's life. He himself mentions the fifteenth year of the reign of Severus as the time when he was writing the work: "Ad xv. jam Severi imperatoris." This agrees with Jerome's Chronicle, where occurs this note: "Anno 2223 Severi xv° Tertullianus...celebratur." This year is assigned to the year of our Lord 207; but notwithstanding the certainty of this date, it is far from clear that it describes more than the time of the publication of *the first book*. On the contrary, it is nearly certain that the other books, although connected manifestly enough in the author's argument and purpose (compare the initial and the final chapters of the several books), were yet issued at separate times. Noesselt shows that between the Book i. and Books ii.–iv. Tertullian issued his *De Præscript. Hæret.*, and previous to Book v. he published his tracts, *De Carne Christi* and *De Resurrectione Carnis*. After giving the incontestable date of the xv. of Severus for the first book, he says it is a mistake to suppose that the other books were published with it. He adds: "Although we cannot undertake to determine whether Tertullian issued his Books ii., iii., iv., against Marcion, together or separately, or in what year, we yet venture to affirm that Book v. appeared apart from the rest. For the tract *De Resurr. Carnis* appears from its second chapter to have been published after the tract *De Carne Christi*, in which latter work (chap. vii.) he quotes a passage from the fourth book against Marcion. But in his Book v. against Marcion (chap. x.), he refers to his work *De Resurr. Carnis*; which circumstance makes it evident that Tertullian published his Book v. at a different time from his Book iv. In his Book i. he announces his intention (chap. i.) of some time or other completing his tract *De Præscript. Hæret.*, but in his book *De Carne Christi* (chap. ii.), he mentions how he had completed it,—a conclusive proof that his Book i. against Marcion preceded the other books."

(III.) Respecting Marcion himself, the most formidable heretic who had as yet opposed revealed truth, enough will turn up in this treatise, with the notes which we have added in explanation, to satisfy the reader. It will, however, be convenient to give here a few introductory particulars of him. Tertullian mentions Marcion as being, with Valentinus, in communion with the Church at Rome, "under the episcopate of the blessed Eleutherus." He goes on to charge them with "ever-restless curiosity, with which they infected even the brethren;" and informs us that they were more than once put out of communion—"Marcion, indeed, with the 200 sesterces which he brought into the church." He goes on to say, that "being at last condemned to the banishment of a perpetual separation, they sowed abroad the poisons of their doctrines. Afterwards, when Marcion, having professed penitence, agreed to the terms offered to him, that he should receive reconciliation on condition that he brought back to the church the rest also, whom he had trained up for perdition, he was prevented by death." He was a native of Sinope in Pontus, of which city, according to an account preserved by Epiphanius, which, however, is somewhat doubtful, his father was bishop, and of high character both for his orthodoxy and exemplary practice. He came to Rome soon after the death of Hyginus, probably about a.d. 141 or 142; and soon after his arrival he adopted the heresy of Cerdon.

(IV.) It is an interesting question as to what edition of the Holy Scriptures Tertullian used in his very copious quotations. It may at once be asserted that he did not cite from the Hebrew, although some writers have claimed for him, among his varied learning, a knowledge of the sacred language. Bp. Kaye observes, page 61, n. 1, that "he sometimes speaks as if he was acquainted with Hebrew," and refers to the *Anti-Marcion* iv. 39, the *Adv. Praxeam* v., and the *Adv. Judæos* ix. Be this as it may, it is manifest that Tertullian's Scripture passages never resemble the Hebrew, but in nearly every instance the Septuagint, whenever, as is most frequently the case, that version differs from the original. In the New Testament there is, as might be expected, a tolerably close conformity to the Greek. There is, however, it must be allowed, a sufficiently frequent variation from the letter of both the Greek Testaments to justify Semler's suspicion that Tertullian always quoted from the old Latin version, whatever that might have been, which was current in the African church in the second and third centuries. The most valuable part of Semler's *Dissertatio de varia et incerta indole Librorum Q. S. F. Tertulliani* is his investigation of this very point. In section iv. he endeavors to prove this proposition: "Hic scriptor non in manibus habuit Græcos libros sacros;" and he states his conclusion thus: "Certissimum est nec Tertullianum nec Cyprianum nec ullum scriptorem e Latinis illis ecclesiasticis provocare unquam ad Græcorum librorum auctoritatem

si vel maxime obscura aut contraria lectio occurreret;" and again: "Ex his satis certum est, Latinos satis diu secutos fuisse auctoritatem suorum librorum adversus Græcos, nec

concessisse nisi serius, cum Augustini et Hieronymi nova auctoritas juvare videretur." It is not ignorance of Greek which is imputed to Tertullian, for he is said to have well understood that language, and even to have composed in it. He probably followed the Latin, as writers now usually quote the authorized English, as being current and best known among their readers. Independent feeling, also, would have weight with such a temper as Tertullian's, to say nothing of the suspicion which largely prevailed in the African branch of the Latin church, that the Greek copies of the Scriptures were much corrupted by the heretics, who were chiefly, if not wholly, Greeks or Greek-speaking persons.

(V.) Whatever perverting effect Tertullian's secession to the sect of Montanus may have had on his judgment in his latest writings, it did not vitiate the work against Marcion. With a few trivial exceptions, this treatise may be read by the strictest Catholic without any feeling of annoyance. His lapse to Montanism is set down conjecturally as having taken place a.d. 199. Jerome, we have seen, attributed the event to his quarrel with the Roman clergy, but this is at least doubtful; nor must it be forgotten that Tertullian's mind seems to have been peculiarly suited by nature to adopt the mystical notions and ascetic principles of Montanus. It is satisfactory to find that, on the whole, "the authority of Tertullian," as the learned Dr. Burton says, "upon great points of doctrine is considered to be little, if at all, affected by his becoming a Montanist." (*Lectures on Eccl. Hist.* vol. ii. p. 234.) Besides the different works which are expressly mentioned in the notes of this volume, recourse has been had by the translator to Dupin's *Hist. Eccl. Writers* (trans.), vol. i. pp. 69–86; Tillemont's *Mèmoires Hist. Eccl.* iii. 85–103; Dr. Smith's *Greek and Roman Biography*, articles "Marcion" and "Tertullian;" Schaff's article, in Herzog's *Cyclopædia,* on "Tertullian;" Munter's *Primordia Eccl. Africanæ,* pp. 118–150; Robertson's *Church Hist.* vol. i. pp. 70–77; Dr. P. Schaff's *Hist. of Christian Church* (New York, 1859, pp. 511–519), and Archdeacon Evans' *Biography of the Early Church,* vol. i. (Lives of "Marcion," pp. 93–122, and "Tertullian," pp. 325–363). This last work, though of a popular cast, shows a good deal of research and learning, expressed in the pleasant style of the once popular author of *The Rectory of Vale Head.* The translator has mentioned these works, because they are all quite accessible to the general reader, and will give him adequate information concerning the subject treated in the present volume.

To this introduction of Dr. Holmes must be added that of Mr. Thelwall, the translator of the Third volume in the Edinburgh Series, as follows:

To arrange chronologically the works (especially if numerous) of an author whose own date is known with tolerable precision, is not always or necessarily easy: witness the controversies as to the succession of St. Paul's epistles. To do this in the case of an author whose own date is itself a matter of controversy may therefore be reasonably expected to be still less so; and such is the predicament of him who attempts to perform this task for Tertullian. I propose to give a specimen or two of the difficulties with which the task is beset; and then to lay before the reader briefly a summary of the results at which eminent scholars, who have devoted much time and thought to the subject, have arrived. Such a course, I think, will at once afford him means of judging of the absolute impossibility of arriving at definite certainty in the matter; and induce him to excuse me if I prefer furnishing him with materials from which to deduce his own conclusions, rather than venturing on an *ex cathedra* decision on so doubtful a subject.

I. The book, as Dr. Holmes has reminded us, of the date of which we seem to have the surest evidence, is *Adv. Marc.* i. This book was in course of writing, as its author himself (c. 15) tells us, "in the fifteenth year of the empire of Severus." Now this date would be clear if there were no doubt as to which year of our era corresponds to Tertullian's fifteenth of Severus. Pamelius, however, says Dr. Holmes, makes it a.d. 208; Clinton, (whose authority is more recent and better,) 207.

2. Another book which promises to give some clue to its date is the *de Pallio*. The writer uses these phrases: "præsentis imperii *triplex virtus;*" "Deo *tot Augustis in unum* favente;" which show that there were at the time three persons unitedly bearing the title *Augusti*—not *Cæsares* only, but the still higher *Augusti*;—while the remainder of that context, as well as the opening of c. 1, indicates a time of peace of some considerable duration; a time of plenty; and a time during and previous to which great changes had taken place in the general aspect of the Roman Empire, and some particular traitor had been discovered and frustrated. Such a combination of circumstances might seem to fix the date with some degree of assurance. But unhappily, as Kaye reminds us, commentators cannot agree as to who the three Augusti are. Some say

Severus, Caracalla, and *Albinus*; some say Severus, Caracalla, and *Geta*. Hence we have a difference of some twelve years or thereabouts in the computations. For Albinus was defeated by Severus in person, and fell by his own hand, in a.d. 197; and Geta, Severus' second son, brother of Caracalla, was not associated by his father with himself and his other son as *Augustus* until a.d. 208, though he had received the title of *Cæsar* ten years before, in the same year in which *Caracalla* had received that of Augustus. For my own part, I may perhaps be allowed to say that I should incline to agree, like Salmasius, with those who assign the later date. The limits of the present Introduction forbid my entering at large into my reasons for so doing. I am, however, supported in it by the authority of Neander. In one point, though, I should hesitate to agree with Oehler, who appears to follow Salmasius and others herein,— namely, in understanding the expression "et cacto et rubo subdolæ familiaritatis convulso" of *Albinus*. It seems to me the words might with more propriety be applied to *Plautianus*; and that in the word "familiaritatis" we may see (after Tertullian's fashion) a play upon the meaning, with a reference not only to the long-standing but mischievous *intimacy* which existed between Severus and his countryman (perhaps fellow-townsman) Plautianus, who for his harshness and cruelty is fitly compared to the prickly *cactus*. He alludes likewise to the alliance which this ambitious prætorian præfect had contrived to contract with the *family* of the emperor, by the marriage of his daughter Plautilla to Caracalla,—an event which, as it turned out, led to his own death. Thus in the "*rubo*" there may be a reference to the ambitious and conceited "bramble" of Jotham's parable, and perhaps, too, to the "thistle" of Jehoash's. If this be so, the date would be at least approximately fixed, as Plautianus did not marry his daughter to Caracalla till a.d. 203, and was himself put to death in the following year, 204, while Geta, as we have seen, was made Augustus in 208.

3. The date of the *Apology*, however, is perhaps at once the most contested, and the most strikingly illustrative of the

difficulties to which allusion has been made. It is not surprising that its date *should* have been more disputed than that of other pieces, inasmuch as it is the best known, and (for some reasons) the most interesting and famous, of all our author's productions. In fact, the dates assigned to it by different authorities vary from Mosheim's 198 to that suggested by the very learned Allix, who assigns it to 217.

4. Once more. In the tract *de Monogamia* (c. 3) the author says that since the date of St. Paul's first Epistle to the Corinthians "about 160 years had elapsed." Here, again, did we only know with certainty the precise date of that epistle, we could ascertain "about" the date of the tract. But (a) the date of the epistle is itself variously given, Burton giving it as early as a.d. 52, Michaelis and Mill as late as 57; and (b) Tertullian only says, "Armis *circiter* clx. exinde productis;" while the way in which, in the *ad Natt.*, within the short space of three chapters, he states first that 250, and then (in c. 9) that 300, years had not elapsed since the rise of the Christian name, leads us to think that here again he only desires to speak in round numbers, meaning perhaps *more* than 150, but *less* than 170.

These specimens must suffice, though it might be easy to add to them. There is, however, another classification of our author's writings which has been attempted. Finding the haplessness of strict chronological accuracy, commentators have seized on the idea that peradventure there might be found at all events some internal marks by which to determine which of them were written before, which after, the writer's secession to Montanism. It may be confessed that this attempt has been somewhat more successful than the other. Yet even here there are two formidable obstacles standing in our way. The first and greatest is, that the natural temper of Tertullian was from the first so akin to the spirit of Montanism, that, unless there occur distinct allusions to the "New Prophecy," or expressions specially connected with Montanistic phraseology, the *general tone* of any treatise is not a very safe guide. The second is, that the subject-matter of some of the treatises is not such as to afford much scope for the introduction of the peculiarities of a sect which professed to differ in discipline only, not doctrine, from the church at large.

Still the result of this classification seems to show one important feature of agreement between commentators, however they may differ upon details; and that is, that considerably the larger part of our author's rather voluminous productions must have been subsequent to his lamented secession. I think the best way to give the reader means for forming his own judgment will be, as I have said, to lay before him in parallel columns a tabular view of the disposition of the books by Dr. Neander and Bishop Kaye. These two modern writers, having given particular care to the subject, bringing to bear upon it all the advantages derived from wide reading, eminent abilities, and a diligent study of the works of preceding writers on the same questions, have a special right to be heard upon the matter in hand; and I think, if I may be allowed to say so, that, for calm judgment, and minute acquaintance with his author, I shall not be accused of undue partiality if I express my opinion that, as far as my own observation goes, the palm must be awarded to the Bishop. In this view I am supported by the fact that the accomplished Professor Ramsay, follows Dr. Kaye's arrangement. I premise that Dr. Neander adopts a threefold division, into:

1. Writings which were occasioned by the relation of the Christians to the heathen, and refer to their vindication of Christianity against the heathen; attacks on heathenism; the sufferings and conduct of Christians under persecution; and the intercourse of Christians with heathens:
2. Writings which relate to Christian and church life, and to ecclesiastical discipline:
3. The dogmatic and dogmatico-controversial treatises.
And under each head he subdivides into:
a. Pre-Montanist writings; b. Post-Montanist writings: thus leaving no room for what Kaye calls "works

respecting which nothing certain can be pronounced." For the sake of clearness, this order has not been followed in the table. On the other side, it will be seen that Dr. Kaye, while not assuming to speak with more than a reasonable probability, is careful so to arrange the treatises under each head as to show the order, so far as it is discoverable, in which the books under that head were published; i.e., if one book is quoted in another book, the book so quoted, if distinctly referred to as already before the world, is plainly anterior to that in which it is quoted. Thus, then, have:

Neander.
I. *Pre-Montanist.*
1. De Poenitentia.
2. De Oratione.
3. De Baptismo.
4. Ad Uxorem i.
5. Ad Uxorem ii.
6. Ad Martyres.
7. De Patientia.
8. De Spectaculis.
9. De Idololatria.
10. 11. Ad Nationes i. ii.
12. Apologeticus.
13. De Testimonio Animæ.
14. De Præscr. Hæreticorum.
15. De Cult. Fem. i.
16. De Cult. Fem. ii.
II. *Montanist.*
17–21. Adv. Marc. i. ii. iii. iv. v.
22. De Anima.
23. De Carne Christi.
24. De Res. Carn.
25. De Cor. Mil.
26. De Virg. Vel.
27. De Ex. Cast.

28. De Monog.
29. De Jejuniis.
30. De Pudicitia.
31. De Pallio.
32. Scorpiace.
33. Ad Scapulam.
34. Adv. Valentinianos.
35. Adv. Hermogenem.
36. Adv. Praxeam.
37. Adv. Judæos.
38. De Fuga in Persecutione.
Kaye.
I. *Pre-Montanist* (probably).
1. De Poenitentia.
2. De Oratione.
3. De Baptismo.
4. Ad Uxorem i.
5. Ad Uxorem ii.
6. Ad Martyres.
7. De Patientia.
8. Adv. Judæos.
9. De Præscr. Hæreticorum.
II. *Montanist* (certainly).
10. Adv. Marc. i.
11. Adv. Marc. ii.
12. De Anima.
13. Adv. Marc. iii.
14. Adv. Marc. iv.
15. De Carne Christi.
16. De Resurrectione Carnis.
17. Adv. Marc. v.
18. Adv. Praxeam.
19. Scorpiace.
20. De Corona Militis.
21. De Virginibus Velandis.
22. De Exhortatione Castitatis.

23. De Fuga in Persecutione.
24. De Monogamia.
25. De Jejuniis.
26. De Pudicitia.
III. *Montanist* (probably).
27. Adv. Valentinianos.
28. Ad Scapulam.
29. De Spectaculis.
30. De Idololatria.
31. De Cultu Feminarum i.
32. De Cultu Feminarum ii.
IV. *Works respecting which nothing certain can be pronounced.*
33. The Apology.
34. Ad Nationes i.
35. Ad Nationes ii.
36. De Testimonio Animæ.
37. De Pallio.
38. Adv. Hermogenem.

A comparison of these two lists will show that the difference between the two great authorities is, as Kaye remarks, "not great; and with respect to some of the tracts on which we differ, the learned author expresses himself with great diffidence." The main difference, in fact, is that which affects two tracts upon kindred subjects, the *de Spectaculis*, and *Idololatria*, the *de Cultu Feminarum* (a subject akin to the other two), and the *adv. Judæos*. With reference to all these, except the last, to which I believe the Archdeacon does not once refer, the Bishop's opinion appears to have the support of Archdeacon Evans, whose learned and interesting essay, referred to in the note, appears in a volume published in 1837. Dr. Kaye's Lectures, on which his book is founded, were delivered in 1825. Of the date of his first edition I am not aware. Dr. Neander's *Antignostikus* also first appeared in 1825. The preface to his second edition bears date July 1, 1849. As to the *adv. Judæos*, I confess I agree with Neander in thinking that, at all events from the beginning of c. 9, it is spurious. If it be urged that Jerome expressly quotes it as Tertullian's, I reply, Jerome so quotes it, I believe, when he is expounding *Daniel*. Now all that the *adv. Jud.* has to say about *Daniel* ends with the end of c. 8. It is therefore quite compatible with the fact thus stated to recognize the earlier half of the book as genuine, and to reject the rest, beginning, as it happens, just after the eighth chapter, as spurious. Perhaps Dr. Neander's Jewish birth and training peculiarly fit him to be heard on this question. Nor do I think Professor Ramsay (in the article above alluded to) has quite seen the force of Kaye's own remarks on Neander.What he does say is equally creditable to his candor and his accuracy; namely: "The instances alleged by Dr. Neander, in proof of this position, are undoubtedly very remarkable; but if the concluding chapters of the tract are spurious, no ground seems to be left for asserting that the genuine portion was posterior to the third Book against Marcion,—and none, consequently, for asserting that it was written by a Montanist." With which remark I must draw these observations on the genuine extant works of Tertullian to a close.

The next point to which a brief reference must be made is the *lost works* of Tertullian, lists of these are given both by Oehler and by Kaye, viz.:

1. A Book on Aaron's Robes: mentioned by Jerome, Epist. 128, *ad Fabiolam de Veste Sacerdotali* (tom. ii. p. 586, Opp. ed. Bened.).
2. A Book on the Superstition of the Age.
3. A Book on the Submission of the Soul.
4. A Book on the Flesh and the Soul.

Nos. 2, 3, and 4 are known only by their titles, which are found in the Index to Tertullian's works given in the *Codex Agobardi*; but the tracts themselves are not extant in the ms., which appears to have once contained—

5. A Book on Paradise, named in the Index, and referred to in *de Anima* 55, *adv. Marc.* iii. 12; and

6. A Book on the Hope of the Faithful: also named in the Index, and referred to *adv. Marc.* iii. 24; and by Jerome in his account of Papias, and on Ezek. xxxvi.; and by Gennadius of Marseilles.

7. Six Books on Ecstasy, with a seventh in reply to Apollonius: see Jerome. See, too, J. A. Fabricius on the words of the unknown author whom the Jesuit Sirmond edited under the name *Prædestinatus*; who gathers thence that "Soter, pope of the City, and Apollonius, bishop of the Ephesians, wrote a book against the Montanists; *in reply to whom* Tertullian, a Carthaginian presbyter, wrote." J. Pamelius thinks these seven books were originally published *in Greek*.

8. A Book in reply to the Apellesites (i.e. the followers of Apelles): referred to in *de Carne Christi*, c. 8.

9. A Book on the Origin of the Soul, in reply to Hermogenes: referred to in *de Anima*, cc. 1, 3, 22, 24.

10. A Book on Fate: referred to by Fulgentius Planciades, p. 562, Merc.; also referred to as either written, or intended to be written, by Tertullian himself, *de Anima*, c. 20. Jerome states that there was extant, or had been extant, a book on Fate under the name of Minucius Felix, written indeed by a perspicuous author, but not in the style of Minucius Felix. This, Pamelius judged, should perhaps be rather ascribed to Tertullian.

11. A Book on the Trinity. Jerome says: "Novatian wrote....a large volume on the Trinity, *as if making an epitome of a work of Tertullian's, which most men not knowing regard it as Cyprian's*." Novatian's book stood in Tertullian's name in the mss. of J. Gangneius, who was the first to edit it; in a Malmesbury ms. which Sig. Gelenius used; and in others.

12. A Book addressed to a Philosophic Friend on the Straits of Matrimony. Both Kaye and Oehler are in doubt whether Jerome's words, by which some have been led to conclude that Tertullian wrote some book or books on this and kindred subjects, really imply as much, or whether they may not refer merely to those tracts and passages in his extant writings which touch upon such matters. Kaye hesitates to

think that the "Book to a Philosophic Friend" is the same as the *de Exhortatione Castitatis*, because Jerome says Tertullian wrote on the subject of celibacy "*in his youth;*" but as Cave takes what Jerome elsewhere says of Tertullian's leaving the Church "*about the middle of his age*" to mean his *spiritual age*, the same sense might attach to his words here too, and thus obviate the Bishop's difficulty.

There are some other works which have been attributed to Tertullian—on Circumcision; on Animals Clean and Unclean; on the truth that God is a Judge—which Oehler likewise rejects, believing that the expressions of Jerome refer only to passages in the *Anti-Marcion* and other extant works. To Novatian Jerome does ascribe a distinct work on Circumcision, and this may (comp. 11, just above) have given rise to the view that Tertullian had written one also.

There were, moreover, three treatises at least written by Tertullian *in Greek*. They are:

1. A Book on Public Shows. See *de Cor*. c. 6.
2. A Book on Baptism. See *de Bapt*. c. 15.
3. A Book on the Veiling of Virgins. See de *V. V.* c. 1.

Oehler adds that J. Pamelius, in his epistle dedicatory to Philip II. of Spain, makes mention of a *Greek copy* of Tertullian in the library of that king. This report, however, since nothing has ever been seen or heard of the said copy from that time, Oehler judges to be erroneous.

It remains briefly to notice the confessedly spurious works which the editions of Tertullian generally have appended to them. With these Kaye does not deal. The fragment, *adv. omnes Hæreses*, Oehler attributes to Victorinus Petavionensis, i.e., Victorinus bishop of Pettaw, on the Drave, in Austrian Styria. It was once thought he ought to be called *Pictaviensis*, i.e. of *Poictiers*; but John Launoy has shown this to be an error. Victorinus is said by Jerome to have "understood Greek better than Latin; hence his works are excellent for the sense, but mean as to the style." Cave believes him to have been a Greek by birth. Cassiodorus states him to have been once a professor of rhetoric. Jerome's statement agrees with the style of the tract in question; and Jerome distinctly says Victorinus did write *adversus omnes Hæreses*. Allix leaves the question of its authorship quite uncertain. If Victorinus be the author, the book falls clearly within the Ante-Nicene period; for Victorinus fell a martyr in the Diocletian persecution, probably about a.d. 303.

The next fragment—"Of the Execrable Gods of the Heathens"—is of quite uncertain authorship. Oehler would attribute it "to some declaimer not quite ignorant of Tertullian's writings," but certainly not to Tertullian himself.

Lastly we come to the metrical fragments. Concerning these, it is perhaps impossible to assign them to their rightful owners. Oehler has not troubled himself much about them; but he seems to regard the *Jonah* as worthy of more regard than the rest, for he seems to have intended giving more labor to its editing at some future time. Whether he has ever done so, or given us his German version of Tertullian's own works, which, "si Deus adjuverit," he distinctly promises in his preface, I do not know. Perhaps the best thing to be done under the circumstances is to give the judgment of the learned Peter Allix. It may be premised that by the celebrated George Fabricius—who published his great work, *Poetarum Veterum Ecclesiasticorum Opera Christiana*, etc., in 1564—the *Five Books in Reply to Marcion*, and the *Judgment of the Lord*, are ascribed to Tertullian, the *Genesis* and *Sodom* to Cyprian.
Pamelius likewise seems to have ascribed the *Five Books*, the *Jonah*, and the *Sodom* to Tertullian; and according to Lardner, Bishop Bull likewise attributed the *Five Books* to him. They have been generally ascribed to the Victorinus above mentioned. Tillemont, among others, thinks they may well enough be his. Rigaltius is content to demonstrate that they are not Tertullian's, but leaves the real authorship without attempting to decide it. Of the others the same eminent critic says, "They seem to have been written at Carthage, at an age not far removed from Tertullian's." Allix, after observing that

Pamelius is inconsistent with himself in attributing the *Genesis* and *Sodom* at one time to Tertullian, at another to Cyprian, rejects both views equally, and assigns the Genesis with some confidence to Salvian, a presbyter of Marseilles, whose "floruit" Cave gives *cir.* 440, a contemporary of Gennadius, and a copious author. To this it is, Allix thinks, that Gennadius alludes in his *Catalogue of Illustrious Men*, c. 77.

The *Judgment of the Lord* Allix ascribes to one Verecundus, an African bishop, whose date he finds it difficult to decide exactly. He refers to two of the name: one Bishop of Tunis, whom Victor of Tunis in his chronicle mentions as having died in exile at Chalcedon a.d. 552; the other Bishop of Noba, who visited Carthage with many others a.d. 482, at the summons of King Huneric, to answer there for their faith;— and would ascribe the poem to the former, thinking that he finds an allusion to it in the article upon that Verecundus in the *de Viris Illustribus* of Isidore of Seville. Oehler agrees with him. The *Five Books* Allix seems to hint may be attributed to some imitator of the Victorinus of Pettaw named above.

Oehler attributes them rather to one Victorinus, or Victor, of Marseilles, a rhetorician, who died a.d. 450. He appears in G. Fabricius as Claudius Marius Victorinus, writer of a *Commentary on Genesis*, and an epistle *ad Salomonem Abbata*, both in verse, and of some considerable length.

The Shows, or De Spectaculis.

Chapter I.

Ye Servants of God, about to draw near to God, that you may make solemn consecration of yourselves to Him, seek well to understand the condition of faith, the reasons of the Truth, the laws of Christian Discipline, which forbid among other sins of the world, the pleasures of the public shows. Ye who have testified and confessed that you have done so already, review the subject, that there may be no sinning whether through real or willful ignorance. For such is the power of earthly pleasures, that, to retain the opportunity of still partaking of them, it contrives to prolong a willing ignorance, and bribes knowledge into playing a dishonest part. To both things, perhaps, some among you are allured by the views of the heathens who in this matter are wont to press us with arguments, such as these: (1) That the exquisite enjoyments of ear and eye we have in things external are not in the least opposed to religion in the mind and conscience; and (2) That surely no offence is offered to God, in any human enjoyment, by any of our pleasures, which it is not sinful to partake of in its own time and place, with all due honor and reverence secured to Him. But this is precisely what we are ready to prove: That these things are not consistent with true religion and true obedience to the true God. There are some who imagine that Christians, a sort of people ever ready to die, are trained into the abstinence they practice, with no other object than that of making it less difficult to despise life, the fastenings to it being severed as it were. *They regard it as an art of* quenching all desire for that which, so far as they are concerned, they have emptied of all that is desirable; and so it is thought to be rather a thing of human planning and foresight, than clearly laid down by divine command. It was a grievous

The Shows or De Spectaculis

thing, forsooth, for Christians, while continuing in the enjoyment of pleasures so great, to die for God! It is not as they say; though, if it were, even Christian obstinacy might well give all submission to a plan so suitable, to a rule so excellent.

Chapter II.

Then, again, everyone is ready with the argument that all things, as we teach, were created by God, and given to man for his use, and that they must be good, as coming all from so good a source; but that among them are found the various constituent elements of the public shows, such as the horse, the lion, bodily strength, and musical voice. It cannot, then, be thought that what exists by God's own creative will is either foreign or hostile to Him; and if it is not opposed to Him, it cannot be regarded as injurious to His worshippers, as certainly it is not foreign to them. Beyond all doubt, too, the very buildings connected with the places of public amusement, composed as they are of rocks, stones, marbles, pillars, are things of God, who has given these various things for the earth's embellishment; nay, the very scenes are enacted under God's own heaven. How skilful a pleader seems human wisdom to herself, especially if she has the fear of losing any of her delights—any of the sweet enjoyments of worldly existence! In fact, you will find not a few whom the imperiling of their pleasures rather than their life holds back from us. For even the weakling has no strong dread of death *as a debt* he knows is due by him; while the wise man does not look with contempt on pleasure, regarding it as a precious gift—in fact, the one blessedness of life, whether to philosopher or fool. Now nobody denies what nobody is ignorant of—for
Nature herself is teacher of it—that God is the Maker of the universe, and that it is good, and that it is man's by free gift of its Maker. But having no intimate acquaintance with the Highest, knowing Him only by natural revelation, and not as His "friends"—afar off, and not as those who have been

brought nigh to Him—men cannot but be in ignorance alike of what He enjoins and what He forbids in regard to the administration of His world. They must be ignorant, too, of the hostile power which works against Him, and perverts to wrong uses the things His hand has formed; for you cannot know either the will or the adversary of a God you do not know. We must not, then, consider merely by whom all things were made, but by whom they have been perverted. We shall find out for what use they were made at first, when we find for what they were not. There is a vast difference between the corrupted state and that of primal purity, just because there is a vast difference between the Creator and the corrupter. Why, all sorts of evils, which as indubitably evils even the heathens prohibit, and against which they guard themselves, come from the works of God. Take, for instance, murder, whether committed by iron, by poison, or by magical enchantments. Iron and herbs and demons are all equally creatures of God. Has the Creator, withal, provided these things for man's destruction? Nay, He puts His interdict on every sort of man-killing by that one summary precept, "Thou shalt not kill." Moreover, who but God, the Maker of the world, put in its gold, brass, silver, ivory, wood, and all the other materials used in the manufacture of idols? Yet has He done this that men may set up a worship in opposition to Himself? On the contrary idolatry in His eyes is the crowning sin. What is there offensive to God which is not God's? But in offending Him, it ceases to be His; and in ceasing to be His, it is in His eyes an offending thing. Man himself, guilty as he is of every iniquity, is not only a work of God—he is His image, and yet both in soul and body he has severed himself from his Maker. For we did not get eyes to minister to lust, and the tongue for speaking evil with, and ears to be the receptacle of evil speech, and the throat to serve the vice of gluttony, and the belly to be gluttony's ally, and the genitals for unchaste excesses, and hands for deeds of violence, and the feet for an erring life; or was the soul placed in the body that it might become a thought-manufactory of snares, and fraud, and injustice? I think not; for if God, as the righteous ex-actor of innocence, hates everything like malignity—if He hates utterly such plotting of evil, it is clear beyond a doubt, that, of all things that have come from His hand, He has made none to lead to works which He condemns, even though these same works may be carried on by things of His making; for, in fact, it is the one ground of condemnation, that the creature misuses the creation. We, therefore, who in our knowledge of the Lord have obtained some knowledge also of His foe—who, in our discovery of the Creator, have at the same time laid hands upon the great corrupter, ought neither to wonder nor to doubt that, as the prowess of the corrupting and God-opposing angel overthrew in the beginning the virtue of man, the work and image of God, the possessor of the world, so he has entirely changed man's nature—created, like his own, for perfect sinlessness—into his own state of wicked enmity against his Maker, that in the very thing whose gift to man, but not to him, had grieved him, he might make man guilty in God's eyes, and set up his own supremacy.

Chapter III.

Fortified by this knowledge against heathen views, let us rather turn to the unworthy reasonings of our own people; for the faith of some, either too simple or too scrupulous, demands direct authority from Scripture for giving up the shows, and holds out that the matter is a doubtful one, because such abstinence is not clearly and in words imposed upon God's servants. Well, we never find it expressed with the same precision, "Thou shalt not enter circus or theatre, thou shalt not look on combat or show;" as it is plainly laid down, "Thou shalt not kill; thou shalt not worship an idol; thou shalt not commit adultery or fraud." But we find that that first word of David bears on this very sort of thing: "Blessed," he says, "is the man who has not gone into the assembly of the impious, nor stood in the way of sinners, nor sat in the seat of scorners."

Though he seems to have predicted beforehand of that just man, that he took no part in the meetings and deliberations of the Jews, taking counsel about the slaying of our Lord, yet divine Scripture has ever far-reaching applications: after the immediate sense has been exhausted, in all directions it fortifies the practice of the religious life, so that here also you have an utterance which is not far from a plain interdicting of the shows. If he called those few Jews an assembly of the wicked, how much more will he so designate so vast a gathering of heathens! Are the heathens less impious, less sinners, less enemies of Christ, than the Jews were then? And see, too, how other things agree. For at the shows they also stand in the way. For they call the spaces between the seats going around the amphitheatre, and the passages which separate the people running down, ways. The place in the curve where the matrons sit is called a chair. Therefore, on the contrary, it holds, unblessed is he who has entered any council of wicked men, and has stood in any way of sinners, and has sat in any chair of scorners. We may understand a thing as spoken generally, even when it requires a certain special interpretation to be given to it. For some things spoken with a special reference contain in them general truth. When God admonishes the Israelites of their duty, or sharply reproves them, He has surely a reference to all men; when He threatens destruction to Egypt and Ethiopia, He surely pre-condemns every sinning nation, whatever. If, reasoning from *species* to *genus*, every nation that sins against them is an Egypt and Ethiopia; so also, reasoning from genus to species, with reference to the origin of shows, every show is an assembly of the wicked.

Chapter IV.

Lest anyone think that we are dealing in mere argumentative subtleties, I shall turn to that highest authority of our "seal" itself. When entering the water, we make profession of the Christian faith in the words of its rule; we bear public testimony that we have renounced the devil, his pomp, and his angels. Well, is it not in connection with idolatry, above all, that you have the devil with his pomp and his angels? from which, to speak briefly—for I do not wish to dilate—you have every unclean and wicked spirit. If, therefore, it shall be made plain that the entire apparatus of the shows is based upon idolatry, beyond all doubt that will carry with it the conclusion that our renunciatory testimony in the laver of baptism has reference to the shows, which, through their idolatry, have been given over to the devil, and his pomp, and his angels. We shall set forth, then, their several origins, in what nursingplaces they have grown to manhood; next the titles of some of them, by what names they are called; then their apparatus, with what superstitions they are observed; (then their places, to what patrons they are dedicated;) then the arts which minister to them, to what authors they are traced. If any of these shall be found to have had no connection with an idol-god, it will be held as free at once from the taint of idolatry, and as not coming within the range of our baptismal abjuration.

Chapter V.

In the matter of their origins, as these are somewhat obscure and but little known to many among us, our investigations must go back to a remote antiquity, and our authorities be none other than books of heathen literature. Various authors are extant who have published works on the subject. The origin of the games as given by them is this. Timæus tells us that immigrants from Asia, under the leadership of Tyrrhenus, who, in a contest about his native kingdom, had succumbed to his brother, settled down in Etruria. Well, among other superstitious observances under the name of religion, they set up in their new home public shows. The Romans, at their own request, obtain from them skilled performers—the proper seasons—the name too, for it is said they are called *Ludi*, from *Lydi*. And though Varro derives the name of *Ludi* from *Ludus*, that is, from play, as they called the Luperci also *Ludii*, because they ran about making sport; still that sporting of young men belongs, in his view, to festal days and temples, and objects of religious veneration. However, it is of little consequence the origin of the name, when it is certain that the thing springs from idolatry. The Liberalia, under the general designation of Ludi, clearly declared the glory of Father Bacchus; for to Bacchus these festivities were first consecrated by grateful peasants, in return for the boon he conferred on them, as they say, making known the pleasures of wine. Then the Consualia were called *Ludi*, and at first were in honor of Neptune, for Neptune has the name of Consus also. Thereafter Romulus dedicated the Equiria to Mars, though they claim the Consualia too for Romulus, on the ground that he consecrated them to Consus, the god, as they will have it, of counsel; of the counsel, forsooth, in which he planned the rape of the Sabine virgins for wives to his soldiers. An excellent counsel truly; and still I suppose reckoned just and righteous by the Romans themselves, I may not say by God. This goes also to taint the origin: you cannot surely hold that to be good which has sprung from sin, from shamelessness, from violence, from hatred, from a fratricidal founder, from a son of Mars. Even now, at the first turning-post in the circus, there is a subterranean altar to this same Consus, with an inscription to this effect: "Consus, great in counsel, Mars, in battle mighty tutelar deities." The priests of the state sacrifice at it on the nones of July; the priest of Romulus and the Vestals on the twelfth before the Kalends of September. In addition to this, Romulus instituted games in honor of Jupiter Feretrius on the Tarpeian Hill, according to the statement Piso has handed down to us, called both Tarpeian and Capitoline. After him Numa Pompilius instituted games to Mars and Robigo (for they have also invented a goddess of rust); then Tullus Hostilius; then Ancus Martius; and various others in succession did the like. As to the idols in whose honor these games were established, ample information is to be found in the pages of Suetonius Tranquillus. But we need say no more to prove the accusation of idolatrous origin.

Chapter VI.

To the testimony of antiquity is added that of later games instituted in their turn, and betraying their origin from the titles which they bear even at the present day, in which it is imprinted as on their very face, for what idol and for what religious object games, whether of the one kind or the other, were designed. You have festivals bearing the name of *the great Mother* and Apollo of Ceres too, and Neptune, and Jupiter Latiaris, and Flora, all celebrated for a common end; the others have their religious origin in the birthdays and solemnities of kings, in public successes in municipal holidays. There are also testamentary exhibitions, in which funeral honors are rendered to the memories of private persons; and this according to an institution of ancient times. For from the first the "Ludi" were regarded as of two sons, sacred and funereal, that is in honor of the heathen deities and of the dead. But in the matter of idolatry, it makes no difference with us under what name or title it is practiced, while it has to do with the wicked spirits whom we abjure. If it is lawful to offer homage to the dead, it will be just as lawful to offer it to their gods: you have the same origin in both cases; there is the same idolatry; there is on our part the same solemn renunciation of all idolatry.

Chapter VII.

The two kinds of public games, then, have one origin; and they have common names, as owning the same parentage. So, too, as they are equally tainted with the sin of idolatry, their foundress, they must need be like each other in their pomp. But the more ambitious preliminary display of the circus games to which the name procession specially belongs, is in itself the proof to whom the whole thing appertains, in the many images the long line of statues, the chariots of all sorts, the thrones, the crowns, the dresses. What high religious rites besides, what sacrifices precede, come between, and follow. How many guilds, how many priesthoods, how many offices are set astir, is known to the inhabitants of the great city in which the demon convention has its headquarters. If these things are done in humbler style in the provinces, in accordance with their inferior means, still all circus games must be counted as belonging to that from which they are derived; the fountain from which they spring defiles them. The tiny streamlet from its very spring-head, the little twig from its very budding, contains in it the essential nature of its origin. It may be grand or mean, no matter, any circus procession whatever is offensive to God. Though there be few images to grace it, there is idolatry in one; though there be no more than a single sacred car, it is a chariot of Jupiter: anything of idolatry whatever, whether meanly arrayed or modestly rich and gorgeous, taints it in its origin.

Chapter VIII.

To follow out my plan in regard to places: the circus is chiefly consecrated to the Sun, whose temple stands in the middle of it, and whose image shines forth from its temple summit; for they have not thought it proper to pay sacred honors underneath a roof to an object they have itself in open space. Those who assert that the first spectacle was exhibited by Circe, and in honor of the Sun her father, as they will have it, maintain also the name of circus was derived from her. Plainly, then, the enchantress did this in the name of the parties whose priestess she was—I mean the demons and spirits of evil. What an aggregation of idolatries you see, accordingly, in the decoration of the place! Every ornament of the circus is a temple by itself. The eggs are regarded as sacred to the Castors, by men who are not ashamed to profess faith in their

The Shows or De Spectaculis

production from the egg of a swan, which was no other than Jupiter himself. The Dolphins vomit forth in honor of Neptune. Images of Sessia, so called as the goddess of sowing; of Messia, so called as the goddess of reaping; of Tutulina, so called as the fruit-protecting deity—load the pillars. In front of these you have three altars to these three gods—Great, Mighty, Victorious. They reckon these of Samo-Thrace. The huge Obelisk, as Hermeteles affirms, is set up in public to the Sun; its inscription, like its origin, belongs to Egyptian superstition. Cheerless were the demon-gathering without their *Mater Magna*; and so she presides there over the Euripus. Consus, as we have mentioned, lies hidden under ground at the Murcian Goals. These two sprang from an idol. For they will have it that Murcia is the goddess of love; and to her, at that spot, they have consecrated a temple. See, Christian, how many impure names have taken possession of the circus! You have nothing to do with a sacred place which is tenanted by such multitudes of diabolic spirits. And speaking of places, this is the suitable occasion for some remarks in anticipation of a point that some will raise. What, then, you say; shall I be in danger of pollution if I go to the circus when the games are not being celebrated? There is no law forbidding the mere places to us. For not only the places for show-gatherings, but even the temples, may be entered without any peril of his religion by the servant of God, if he has only some honest reason for it, unconnected with their proper business and official duties. Why, even the streets and the market-place, and the baths, and the taverns, and our very dwelling-places, are not altogether free from idols. Satan and his angels have filled the whole world. It is not by merely being in the world, however, that we lapse from God, but by touching and tainting ourselves with the world's sins. I shall break with my Maker, that is, by going to the Capitol or the temple of Serapis to sacrifice or adore, as I shall also do by going as a spectator to the circus and the theatre. The places in themselves do not contaminate, but what is done in them; from this even the places themselves, we maintain, become defiled. The polluted things pollute us. It is on this account that we set before you to whom places of the kind are dedicated, that we may prove the things which are done in them to belong to the idol patrons to whom the very places are sacred.

Chapter IX.

Now as to the kind of performances peculiar to the circus exhibitions. In former days equestrianism was practiced in a simple way on horseback, and certainly its ordinary use had nothing sinful in it; but when it was dragged into the games, it passed from the service of God into the employment of demons. Accordingly this kind of circus performances is regarded as sacred to Castor and Pollux, to whom, Stesichorus tells us, horses were given by Mercury. And Neptune, too, is an equestrian deity, by the Greeks called Hippius. In regard to the team, they have consecrated the chariot and four to the sun; the chariot and pair to the moon. But, as the poet has it, "Erichthonius first dared to yoke four horses to the chariot, and to ride upon its wheels with victorious swiftness." Erichthonius, the son of Vulcan and Minerva, fruit of unworthy passion upon earth, is a demon-monster, nay, the devil himself, and no mere snake. But if Trochilus the Argive is maker of the first chariot, he dedicated that work of his to Juno. If Romulus first exhibited the four-horse chariot at Rome, he too, I think, has a place given him among idols, at least if he and Quirinus are the same. But as chariots had such inventors, the charioteers were naturally dressed, too, in the colors of idolatry; for at first these were only two, namely white and red,—the former sacred to the winter with its glistening snows, the latter sacred to the summer with its ruddy sun: but afterwards, in the progress of luxury as well as of superstition, red was dedicated by some to Mars, and white by others to the Zephyrs, while green was given to Mother Earth, or spring, and azure to the sky and sea, or autumn. But as idolatry of every kind is condemned by God, that form of it surely shares the condemnation which is offered to the elements of nature.

Chapter X.

Let us pass on now to theatrical exhibitions, which we have already shown have a common origin with the circus, and bear like idolatrous designations—even as from the first they have borne the name of "Ludi," and equally minister to idols. They resemble each other also in their pomp, having the same procession to the scene of their display from temples and altars, and that mournful profusion of incense and blood, with music of pipes and trumpets, all under the direction of the soothsayer and the undertaker, those two foul masters of funeral rites and sacrifices. So as we went on from the origin of the "Ludi" to the circus games, we shall now direct our course thence to those of the theatre, beginning with the place of exhibition. At first the theatre was properly a temple of Venus; and, to speak briefly, it was owing to this that stage performances were allowed to escape censure, and got a footing in the world. For ofttimes the censors, in the interests of morality, put down above all the rising theatres, foreseeing, as they did, that there was great danger of their leading to a general profligacy; so that already, from this accordance of their own people with us, there is a witness to the heathen, and in the anticipatory judgment of human knowledge even a confirmation of our views. Accordingly Pompey the Great, less only than his theatre, when he had erected that citadel of all impurities, fearing some time or other censorian condemnation of his memory, superposed on it a temple of Venus; and summoning by public proclamation the people to its consecration, he called it not a theatre, but a temple, "under which," said he, "we have placed tiers of seats for viewing the shows." So he threw a veil over a structure on which condemnation had been often passed, and which is ever to be held in reprobation, by pretending that it was a sacred place; and by means of superstition he blinded the eyes of a virtuous discipline. But Venus and Bacchus are close allies. These two evil spirits are in sworn confederacy with each other, as the patrons of drunkenness and lust. So the theatre of Venus is as well the house of Bacchus: for they properly gave the name of Liberalia also to other theatrical amusements—which besides being consecrated to Bacchus (as were the Dionysia of the Greeks), were instituted by him; and, without doubt, the performances of the theatre have the common patronage of these two deities. That immodesty of gesture and attire which so specially and peculiarly characterizes the stage are consecrated to them—the one deity wanton by her sex, the other by his drapery; while its services of voice, and song, and lute, and pipe, belong to Apollos, and Muses, and Minervas, and Mercuries. You will hate, O Christian, the things whose authors must be the objects of your utter detestation. So we would now make a remark about the arts of the theatre, about the things also whose authors in the names we execrate. We know that the names of the dead are nothing, as are their images; but we know well enough, too, who, when images are set up, under these names carry on their wicked work, and exult in the homage rendered to them, and pretend to be divine—none other than spirits accursed, than devils. We see, therefore, that the arts also are consecrated to the service of the beings who dwell in the names of their founders; and that things cannot be held free from the taint of idolatry whose inventors have got a place among the gods for their discoveries. Nay, as regards the arts, we ought to have gone further back, and barred all further argument by the position that the demons, predetermining in their own interests from the first, among other evils of idolatry, the pollutions of the public shows, with the object of drawing man away from his Lord and binding him to their own service, carried out their purpose by bestowing on him the artistic gifts which the shows require. For none but themselves would have made provision and preparation for the objects they had in view; nor would they have given the arts to the world by any but those in whose names, and images, and histories they set up for their own ends the artifice of consecration.

Chapter XI.

In fulfillment of our plan, let us now go on to consider the combats. Their origin is akin to that of the games (*ludi*). Hence they are kept as either sacred or funereal, as they have been instituted in honor of the idol-gods of the nations or of the dead. Thus, too, they are called Olympian in honor of Jupiter, known at Rome as the Capitoline; Nemean, in honor of Hercules; Isthmian, in honor of Neptune; the rest *mortuarii*, as belonging to the dead. What wonder, then, if idolatry pollutes the combat-parade with profane crowns, with sacerdotal chiefs, with attendants belonging to the various colleges, last of all with the blood of its sacrifices? To add a completing word about the "place"—in the common place for the college of the arts sacred to the Muses, and Apollo, and Minerva, and also for that of the arts dedicated to Mars, they with contest and sound of trumpet emulate the circus in the arena, which is a real temple—I mean of the god whose festivals it celebrates. The gymnastic arts also originated with their Castors, and Herculeses, and Mercuries.

Chapter XII.

It remains for us to examine the "spectacle" most noted of all, and in highest favor. It is called a dutiful service (*munus*), from its being an office, for it bears the name of "*officium*" as well as "*munus*." The ancients thought that in this solemnity they rendered offices to the dead; at a later period, with a cruelty more refined, they somewhat modified its character. For formerly, in the belief that the souls of the departed were appeased by human blood, they were in the habit of buying captives or slaves of wicked disposition, and immolating them in their funeral obsequies. Afterwards they thought good to throw the veil of pleasure over their iniquity. Those, therefore, whom they had provided for the combat, and then trained in arms as best they could, only that they might learn to die, they, on the funeral day, killed at the places of sepulture. They alleviated death by murders. Such is the origin of the "Munus." But by degrees their refinement came up to their cruelty; for these human wild beasts could not find pleasure exquisite enough, save in the spectacle of men torn to pieces by wild beasts. Offerings to propitiate the dead then were regarded as belonging to the class of funeral sacrifices; and these are idolatry: for idolatry, in fact, is a sort of homage to the departed; the one as well as the other is a service to dead men. Moreover, demons have abode in the images of the dead. To refer also to the matter of names, though this sort of exhibition has passed from honors of the dead to honors of the living, I mean, to quæstorships and magistracies—to priestly offices of different kinds; yet, since idolatry still cleaves to the dignity's name, whatever is done in its name partakes of its impurity. The same remark will apply to the procession of the "Munus," as we look at that in the pomp which is connected with these honors themselves; for the purple robes, the fasces, the fillets, the crowns, the proclamations too, and edicts, the sacred feasts of the day before, are not without the pomp of the devil, without invitation of demons. What need, then, of dwelling on the place of horrors, which is too much even for the tongue of the perjurer? For the amphitheatre is consecrated to names more numerous and more dire than is the Capitol itself, temple of all demons as it is. There are as many unclean spirits there as it holds men. To conclude with a single remark about the arts which have a place in it, we know that its two sorts of amusement have for their patrons Mars and Diana.

Chapter XIII.

We have, I think, faithfully carried out our plan of showing in how many different ways the sin of idolatry clings to the shows, in respect of their origins, their titles, their equipments, their places of celebration, their arts; and we may hold it as a thing beyond all doubt, that for us who have twice renounced all idols, they are utterly unsuitable. "Not that an idol is anything," as the apostle says, but that the homage they render is to demons, who are the real occupants of these consecrated images, whether of dead men or (as they think) of gods. On this account, therefore, because they have a common source—for their dead and their deities are one—we abstain from both idolatries. Nor do we dislike the temples less than the monuments: we have nothing to do with either altar, we adore neither image; we do not offer sacrifices to the gods, and we make no funeral oblations to the departed; nay, we do not partake of what is offered either in the one case or the other, for we cannot partake of God's feast and the feast of devils. If, then, we keep throat and belly free from such defilements, how much more do we withhold our nobler parts, our ears and eyes, from the idolatrous and funereal enjoyments, which are not passed through the body, but are digested in the very spirit and soul, whose purity, much more than that of our bodily organs, God has a right to claim from us.

Chapter XIV.

Having sufficiently established the charge of idolatry, which alone ought to be reason enough for our giving up the shows, let us now *ex abundanti* look at the subject in another way, for the sake of those especially who keep themselves comfortable in the thought that the abstinence we urge is not in so many words enjoined, as if in the condemnation of the lusts of the world there was not involved a sufficient declaration against all these amusements. For as there is a lust of money, or rank, or eating, or impure enjoyment, or glory, so there is also a lust of pleasure. But the show is just a sort of pleasure. I think, then, that under the general designation of lusts, pleasures are included; in like manner, under the general idea of pleasures, you have as a specific class the "shows." But we have spoken already of how it is with the places of exhibition, that they are not polluting in themselves, but owing to the things that are done in them from which they imbibe impurity, and then spirt it again on others.

Chapter XV.

Having done enough, then, as we have said, in regard to that principal argument, that there is in them all the taint of idolatry—having sufficiently dealt with that, let us now contrast the other characteristics of the show with the things of God. God has enjoined us to deal calmly, gently, quietly, and peacefully with the Holy Spirit, because these things are alone in keeping with the goodness of His nature, with His tenderness and sensitiveness, and not to vex Him with rage, ill-nature, anger, or grief. Well, how shall this be made to accord with the shows? For the show always leads to spiritual agitation, since where there is pleasure, there is keenness of feeling giving pleasure its zest; and where there is keenness of feeling, there is rivalry giving in turn its zest to that. Then, too, where you have rivalry, you have rage, bitterness, wrath and grief, with all bad things which flow from them—the whole entirely out of keeping with the religion of Christ. For even suppose one should enjoy the shows in a moderate way, as befits his rank, age or nature, still he is not undisturbed in mind, without some unuttered movings of the inner man. No one partakes of pleasures such as these without their strong excitements; no one comes under their excitements without their natural lapses. These lapses, again, create passionate desire. If there is no desire, there is no pleasure, and he is chargeable with trifling who goes where nothing is gotten; in my view, even that is foreign to us. Moreover, a man pronounces his own condemnation in the very act of taking his place among those with whom, by his disinclination to be like them, he confesses he has no sympathy. It is not enough that we do no such things ourselves, unless we break all connection also with those who do. "If thou sawest a thief," says the Scripture, "thou consentedst with him." Would that we did not even inhabit the same world with these wicked men! But though that wish cannot be realized, yet even now we are separate from them in what is of the world; for the world is God's, but the worldly is the devil's.

Chapter XVI.

Since, then, all passionate excitement is forbidden us, we are debarred from every kind of spectacle, and especially from the circus, where such excitement presides as in its proper element. See the people coming to it already under strong emotion, already tumultuous, already passion-blind, already agitated about their bets. The prætor is too slow for them: their eyes are ever rolling as though along with the lots in his urn; then they hang all eager on the signal; there is the united shout of a common madness. Observe how "out of themselves" they are by their foolish speeches. "He has thrown it!" they exclaim; and they announce each one to his neighbor what all have seen. I have clearest evidence of their blindness; they do not see what is really thrown. They think it a "signal cloth," but it is the likeness of the devil cast headlong from on high. And the result accordingly is, that they fly into rages, and passions, and discords, and all that they who are consecrated to peace ought never to indulge in. Then there are curses and reproaches, with no cause of hatred; there are cries of applause, with nothing to merit them. What are the partakers in all this—not their own masters—to obtain of it for themselves? unless, it may be, that which makes them not their own: they are saddened by another's sorrow, they are gladdened by another's joy. Whatever they desire on the one hand, or detest on the other, is entirely foreign to themselves. So love with them is a useless thing, and hatred is unjust. Or is a causeless love perhaps more legitimate than a causeless hatred? God certainly forbids us to hate even with a reason for our hating; for He commands us to love our enemies. God forbids us to curse, though there be some ground for doing so, in commanding that those who curse us we are to bless. But what is more merciless than the circus, where people do not spare even their rulers and fellowcitizens? If any of its madnesses are becoming elsewhere in the saints of God, they will be seemly in the circus too; but if they are nowhere right, so neither are they there.

Chapter XVII.

Are we not, in like manner, enjoined to put away from us all immodesty? On this ground, again, we are excluded from the theatre, which is immodesty's own peculiar abode, where nothing is in repute but what elsewhere is disreputable. So the best path to the highest favor of its god is the vileness which the Atellan gesticulates, which the buffoon in woman's clothes exhibits, destroying all natural modesty, so that they blush more readily at home than at the play, which finally is done from his childhood on the person of the pantomime, that he may become an actor. The very harlots, too, victims of the public lust, are brought upon the stage, their misery increased as being there in the presence of their own sex, from whom alone they are wont to hide themselves: they are paraded publicly before every age and every rank—their abode, their gains, their praises, are set forth, and that even in the hearing of those who should not hear such things. I say nothing about other matters, which it was good to hide away in their own darkness and their own gloomy caves, lest they should stain the light of day. Let the Senate, let all ranks, blush for very shame! Why, even these miserable women, who by their own gestures destroy their modesty, dreading the light of day, and the people's gaze, know something of shame at least once a year. But if we ought to abominate all that is immodest, on what ground is it right to hear what we must not speak? For all licentiousness of speech, nay, every idle word, is condemned by God. Why, in the same way, is it right to look on what it is disgraceful to do? How is it that the things which defile a man in going out of his mouth, are not regarded as doing so when they go in at his eyes and ears—when eyes and ears are the immediate attendants on the spirit—and that can never be pure whose servants-in-waiting are impure? You have the theatre forbidden, then, in the forbidding of immodesty. If, again, we despise the teaching of secular literature as being foolishness in God's eyes, our duty is plain enough in regard to those spectacles, which from this source derive the tragic or comic play. If tragedies and comedies are the bloody and wanton, the impious and licentious inventors of crimes and lusts, it is not good even that there should be any calling to remembrance the atrocious or the vile. What you reject in deed, you are not to bid welcome to in word.

Chapter XVIII.

But if you argue that the racecourse is mentioned in Scripture, I grant it at once. But you will not refuse to admit that the things which are done there are not for you to look upon: the blows, and kicks, and cuffs, and all the recklessness of hand, and everything like that disfiguration of the human countenance, which is nothing less than the disfiguration of God's own image. You will never give your approval to those foolish racing and throwing feats, and yet more foolish leapings; you will never find pleasure in injurious or useless exhibitions of strength; certainly you will not regard with approval those efforts after an artificial body which aim at surpassing the Creator's work; and you will have the very opposite of complacency in the athletes Greece, in the inactivity of peace, feeds up. And the wrestler's art is a devil's thing. The devil wrestled with, and crushed to death, the first human beings. Its very attitude has power in it of the serpent kind, firm to hold—tortures to clasp—slippery to glide away.

You have no need of crowns; why do you strive to get pleasures from crowns?

Chapter XIX.

We shall now see how the Scriptures condemn the amphitheatre. If we can maintain that it is right to indulge in the cruel, and the impious, and the fierce, let us go there. If we are what we are said to be, let us regale ourselves there with human blood. It is good, no doubt, to have the guilty punished. Who but the criminal himself will deny that? And yet the innocent can find no pleasure in another's sufferings: he rather mourns that a brother has sinned so heinously as to need a punishment so dreadful. But who is my guarantee that it is always the guilty who are adjudged to the wild beasts, or to some other doom, and that the guiltless never suffer from the revenge of the judge, or the weakness of the defense, or the pressure of the rack? How much better, then, is it for me to remain ignorant of the punishment inflicted on the wicked, lest I am obliged to know also of the good coming to untimely ends—if I may speak of goodness in the case at all! At any rate, gladiators not chargeable with crime are offered in sale for the games, that they may become the victims of the public pleasure. Even in the case of those who are judicially condemned to the amphitheatre, what a monstrous thing it is, that, in undergoing their punishment, they, from some less serious delinquency, advance to the criminality of manslayers! But I mean these remarks for heathen. As to Christians, I shall not insult them by adding another word as to the aversion with which they should regard this sort of exhibition; though no one is more able than myself to set forth fully the whole subject, unless it be one who is still in the habit of going to the shows. I would rather withal be incomplete than set memory a-working.

Chapter XX.

How vain, then—nay, how desperate—is the reasoning of persons, who, just because they decline to lose a pleasure, hold out that we cannot point to the specific words or the very place where this abstinence is mentioned, and where the servants of God are directly forbidden to have anything to do with such assemblies! I heard lately a novel defense of himself by a certain play-lover. "The sun," said he, "nay, God Himself, looks down from heaven on the show, and no pollution is contracted." Yes, and the sun, too, pours down his rays into the common sewer without being defiled. As for God, would that all crimes were hid from His eye, that we might all escape judgment! But He looks on robberies too; He looks on falsehoods, adulteries, frauds, idolatries, and these same shows; and precisely on that account we will not look on them, lest the All-seeing see us. You are putting on the same level, O man, the criminal and the judge; the criminal who is a criminal because he is seen, and the Judge who is a Judge because He sees. Are we set, then, on playing the madman outside the circus boundaries? Outside the gates of the theatre are we bent on lewdness, outside the course on arrogance, and outside the amphitheatre on cruelty, because outside the porticoes, the tiers and the curtains, too, God has eyes? Never and nowhere is that free from blame which God ever condemns; never and nowhere is it right to do what you may not do at all times and in all places. It is the freedom of the truth from change of opinion and varying judgments which constitutes its perfection, and gives it its claims to full mastery, unchanging reverence, and faithful obedience. That which is really good or really evil cannot be ought else. But in all things the truth of God is immutable.

Chapter XXI.

The heathen, who have not a full revelation of the truth, for they are not taught of God, hold a thing evil and good as it suits self-will and passion, making that which is good in one place evil in another, and that which is evil in one place in another good. So it strangely happens, that the same man who can scarcely in public lift up his tunic, even when necessity of nature presses him, takes it off in the circus, as if bent on exposing himself before everybody; the father who carefully protects and guards his virgin daughter's ears from every polluting word, takes her to the theatre himself, exposing her to all its vile words and attitudes; he, again, who in the streets lays hands on or covers with reproaches the brawling pugilist, in the arena gives all encouragement to combats of a much more serious kind; and he who looks with horror on the corpse of one who has died under the common law of nature, in the amphitheatre gazes down with most patient eyes on bodies all mangled and torn and smeared with their own blood; nay, the very man who comes to the show, because he thinks murderers ought to suffer for their crime, drives the unwilling gladiator to the murderous deed with rods and scourges; and one who demands the lion for every manslayer of deeper dye, will have the staff for the savage swordsman, and rewards him with the cap of liberty. Yes and he must have the poor victim back again, that he may get a sight of his face—with zest inspecting near at hand the man whom he wished torn in pieces at safe distance from him: so much the more cruel he if that was not his wish.

Chapter XXII.

What wonder is there in it? Such inconsistencies as these are just such as we might expect from men, who confuse and change the nature of good and evil in their inconstancy of feeling and fickleness in judgment. Why, the authors and managers of the spectacles, in that very respect with reference to which they highly laud the charioteers, and actors, and wrestlers, and those most loving gladiators, to whom men prostitute their souls, women too their bodies, slight and trample on them, though for their sakes they are guilty of the deeds they reprobate; nay, they doom them to ignominy and the loss of their rights as citizens, excluding them from the Curia, and the rostra, from senatorial and equestrian rank, and from all other honors as well as certain distinctions. What perversity! They have pleasure in those whom yet they punish; they put all slights on those to whom, at the same time, they award their approbation; they magnify the art and brand the artist. What an outrageous thing it is, to blacken a man on account of the very things which make him meritorious in their eyes! Nay, what a confession that the things are evil, when their authors, even in highest favor, are not without a mark of disgrace upon them!

Chapter XXIII.

Seeing, then, man's own reflections, even in spite of the sweetness of pleasure, lead him to think that people such as these should be condemned to a hapless lot of infamy, losing all the advantages connected with the possession of the dignities of life, how much more does the divine righteousness inflict punishment on those who give themselves to these arts! Will God have any pleasure in the charioteer who disquiets so many souls, rouses up so many furious passions, and creates so many various moods, either crowned like a priest or wearing the colors of a pimp, decked out by the devil that he may be whirled away in his chariot, as though with the object of taking off Elijah? Will He be pleased with him who applies the razor to himself, and completely changes his features; who, with no respect for his face, is not content with making it as like as possible to Saturn and Isis and Bacchus, but gives it quietly over to contumelious blows, as if in mockery of our Lord? The devil, forsooth, makes it part, too, of his teaching, that the cheek is to be meekly offered to the smiter. In the same way, with their high shoes, he has made the tragic actors taller, because "none can add a cubit to his stature." His desire is to make Christ a liar. And in regard to the wearing of masks, I ask is that according to the mind of God, who forbids the making of every likeness, and especially then the likeness of man who is His own image? The Author of truth hates all the false; He regards as adultery all that is unreal. Condemning, therefore, as He does hypocrisy in every form, He never will approve any putting on of voice, or sex, or age; He never will approve pretended loves, and wraths, and groans, and tears. Then, too, as in His law it is declared that the man is cursed who attires himself in female garments, what must be His judgment of the pantomime, who is even brought up to play the woman! And will the boxer go unpunished? I suppose he received these cæstus-scars, and the thick skin of his fists, and these growths upon his ears, at his creation! God, too, gave him eyes for no other end than that they might be knocked out in fighting! I say nothing of him who, to save himself, thrusts another in the lion's way, that he may not be too little of a murderer when he puts to death that very same man on the arena.

Chapter XXIV.

In how many other ways shall we yet further show that nothing which is peculiar to the shows has God's approval, or without that approval is becoming in God's servants? If we have succeeded in making it plain that they were instituted entirely for the devil's sake, and have been got up entirely with the devil's things (for all that is not God's, or is not pleasing in His eyes, belongs to His wicked rival), this simply means that in them you have that pomp of the devil which in the "seal" of our faith we abjure. We should have no connection with the things which we abjure, whether in deed or word, whether by looking on them or looking forward to them; but do we not abjure and rescind that baptismal pledge, when we cease to bear its testimony? Does it then remain for us to apply to the heathen themselves. Let them tell us, then, whether it is right in Christians to frequent the show. Why, the rejection of these amusements is the chief sign to them that a man has adopted the Christian faith. If anyone, then, puts away the faith's distinctive badge, he is plainly guilty of denying it. What hope can you possibly retain in regard to a man who does that? When you go over to the enemy's camp, you throw down your arms, desert the standards and the oath of allegiance to your chief: you cast in your lot for life or death with your new friends.

Chapter XXV.

Seated where there is nothing of God, will one be thinking of his Maker? Will there be peace in his soul when there is eager strife there for a charioteer? Wrought up into a frenzied excitement, will he learn to be modest? Nay, in the whole thing he will meet with no greater temptation than that gay attiring of the men and women. The very intermingling of emotions, the very agreements and disagreements with each other in the bestowment of their favors, where you have such close communion, blow up the sparks of passion. And then there is scarce any other object in going to the show, but to see and to be seen. When a tragic actor is declaiming, will one be giving thought to prophetic appeals? Amid the measures of the effeminate player, will he call up to himself a psalm? And when the athletes are hard at struggle, will he be ready to proclaim that there must be no striking again? And with his eye fixed on the bites of bears, and the sponge-nets of the net-fighters, can he be moved by compassion? May God avert from His people any such passionate eagerness after a cruel enjoyment! For how monstrous it is to go from God's church to the devil's—from the sky to the stye, as they say; to raise your hands to God, and then to weary them in the applause of an actor; out of the mouth, from which you uttered Amen over the Holy Thing, to give witness in a gladiator's favor; to cry "forever" to anyone else but God and Christ!

Chapter XXVI.

Why may not those who go into the temptations of the show become accessible also to evil spirits? We have the case of the woman—the Lord Himself is witness—who went to the theatre, and came back possessed. In the outcasting, accordingly, when the unclean creature was upbraided with having dared to attack a believer, he firmly replied, "And in truth I did it most righteously, for I found her in my domain." Another case, too, is well known, in which a woman had been hearing a tragedian, and on the very night she saw in her sleep a linen cloth—the actor's name being mentioned at the same time with strong disapproval—and five days after that woman was no more. How many other undoubted proofs we have had in the case of persons who, by keeping company with the devil in the shows, have fallen from the Lord! For no one can serve two masters. What fellowship has light with darkness, life with death?

Chapter XXVII.

We ought to detest these heathen meetings and assemblies, if on no other account than that there God's name is blasphemed—that there the cry "To the lions!" is daily raised against us—that from thence persecuting decrees are wont to emanate, and temptations are sent forth. What will you do if you are caught in that heaving tide of impious judgments? Not that there any harm is likely to come to you from men: nobody knows that you are a Christian; but think how it fares with you in heaven. For at the very time the devil is working havoc in the church, do you doubt that the angels are looking down from above, and marking every man, who speaks and who listens to the blaspheming word, who lends his tongue and who lends his ears to the service of Satan against God? Shall you not then shun those tiers where the enemies of Christ assemble, that seat of all that is pestilential, and the very super incumbent atmosphere all impure with wicked cries? Grant that you have there things that are pleasant, things both agreeable and

The Shows or De Spectaculis

innocent in themselves; even some things that are excellent. Nobody dilutes poison with gall and hellebore: the accursed thing is put into condiments well seasoned and of sweetest taste. So, too, the devil puts into the deadly draught which he prepares, things of God most pleasant and most acceptable. Everything there, then, that is either brave, noble, loud-sounding, melodious, or exquisite in taste, hold it but as the honey drop of a poisoned cake; nor make so much of your taste for its pleasures, as of the danger you run from its attractions.

Chapter XXVIII.

With such dainties as these let the devil's guests be feasted. The places and the times, the inviter too, are theirs. Our banquets, our nuptial joys, are yet to come. We cannot sit down in fellowship with them, as neither can they with us. Things in this matter go by their turns. Now they have gladness and we are troubled. "The world," says Jesus, "shall rejoice; ye shall be sorrowful." Let us mourn, then, while the heathen is merry, that in the day of their sorrow we may rejoice; lest, sharing now in their gladness, we share then also in their grief. Thou art too dainty, Christian, if thou wouldst have pleasure in this life as well as in the next; nay, a fool thou art, if thou thinkest this life's pleasures to be really pleasures. The philosophers, for instance, give the name of pleasure to quietness and repose; in that they have their bliss; in that they find entertainment: they even glory in it. You long for the goal, and the stage, and the dust, and the place of combat! I would have you answer me this question: Can we not live without pleasure, who cannot but with pleasure die? For what is our wish but the apostle's, to leave the world, and be taken up into the fellowship of our Lord? You have your joys where you have your longings.

Chapter XXIX.

Even as things are, if your thought is to spend this period of existence in enjoyments, how are you so ungrateful as to reckon insufficient, as not thankfully to recognize the many and exquisite pleasures God has bestowed upon you? For what more delightful than to have God the Father and our Lord at peace with us, than revelation of the truth than confession of our errors, than pardon of the innumerable sins of our past life? What greater pleasure than distaste of pleasure itself, contempt of all that the world can give, true liberty, a pure conscience, a contented life, and freedom from all fear of death? What nobler than to tread underfoot the gods of the nations—to exorcise evil spirits—to perform cures—to seek divine revealings—to live to God? These are the pleasures, these the spectacles that befit Christian men—holy, everlasting, free. Count of these as your circus games, fix your eyes on the courses of the world, the gliding seasons, reckon up the periods of time, long for the goal of the final consummation, defend the societies of the churches, be startled at God's signal, be roused up at the angel's trump, glory in the palms of martyrdom. If the literature of the stage delight you, we have literature in abundance of our own—plenty of verses, sentences, songs, proverbs; and these not fabulous, but true; not tricks of art, but plain realities. Would you have also fightings and wrestlings? Well, of these there is no lacking, and they are not of slight account. Behold unchastity overcome by chastity, perfidy slain by faithfulness, cruelty stricken by compassion, impudence thrown into the shade by modesty: these are the contests we have among us, and in these *we* win our crowns. Would you have something of blood too? You have Christ's.

Chapter XXX.

But what a spectacle is that fast-approaching advent of our Lord, now owned by all, now highly exalted, now a triumphant One! What that exultation of the angelic hosts! What the glory of the rising saints! What the kingdom of the

The Shows or De Spectaculis

just thereafter! What the city New Jerusalem! Yes, and there are other sights: that last day of judgment, with its everlasting issues; that day unlooked for by the nations, the theme of their derision, when the world hoary with age, and all its many products, shall be consumed in one great flame! How vast a spectacle then bursts upon the eye! What there excites my admiration? what my derision? Which sight gives me joy? which rouses me to exultation?—as I see so many illustrious monarchs, whose reception into the heavens was publicly announced, groaning now in the lowest darkness with great Jove himself, and those, too, who bore witness of their exultation; governors of provinces, too, who persecuted the Christian name, in fires fiercer than those with which in the days of their pride they raged against the followers of Christ. What world's wise men besides, the very philosophers, in fact, who taught their followers that God had no concern in ought that is sublunary, and were wont to assure them that either they had no souls, or that they would never return to the bodies which at death they had left, now covered with shame before the poor deluded ones, as one fire consumes them!

Poets also, trembling not before the judgment-seat of Rhadamanthus or Minos, but of the unexpected Christ! I shall have a better opportunity then of hearing the tragedians, loudervoiced in their own calamity; of viewing the play-actors, much more "dissolute" in the dissolving flame; of looking upon the charioteer, all glowing in his chariot of fire; of beholding the wrestlers, not in their gymnasia, but tossing in the fiery billows; unless even then I shall not care to attend to such ministers of sin, in my eager wish rather to fix a gaze insatiable on those whose fury vented itself against the Lord. "This," I shall say, "this is that carpenter's or hireling's son, that Sabbath-breaker, that Samaritan and devil-possessed! This is He whom you purchased from Judas! This is He whom you struck with reed and fist, whom you contemptuously spat upon, to whom you gave gall and vinegar to drink! This is He whom His disciples secretly stole away, that it might be said He had risen again, or the gardener abstracted, that his lettuces might come to no harm from the crowds of visitants!" What quæstor or priest in his munificence will bestow on you the favor of seeing and exulting in such things as these? And yet even now we in a measure have them by faith in the picturings of imagination. But what are the things which eye has not seen, ear has not heard, and which have not so much as dimly dawned upon the human heart? Whatever they are, they are nobler, I believe, than circus, and both theatres, and every racecourse.

www.ingramcontent.com/pod-product-compliance
Lightning Source LLC
Chambersburg PA
CBHW052119070526
44584CB00017B/2560